Words of a Tear

Life's Poetry 1

Rodney D. Harakal

Life's Poetry 1

Dedication

These Wordy Expressions of Art Are Dedicated To
My Daughter Trista And My Three Grandbaby Girls

Table of Contents

A Dealt Life

I speak words from the tongue,
That flows through my head.
Some things were done wrong,
And some things were said.

I did not teach you to steal,
Or take things that are not yours.
Precious moments are missing,
Problems you cannot cure.

Jewels of our hands,
And gems of our hearts.
It comes from unknown places,
Replacing them is hard.

Someone stole from you,
And never gave back.
They did not give you a choice,
Or give you any slack.

They taketh and not giveth,
Physical and mind.
They took what was yours,
And returned nothing, so unkind.

Your life was stolen from you,
At a very young age.
Not given to you, were your dad and the grace of his days.

They talked no good,
And gave no credit due.
He left good reason,
And he was very much true to you.

His life is better,
When you believe in him.
He is here for you,
Through the thickest and thin.

Problems came our way,
And alone they need to be dealt,
Times will be hard,
Living each day without.

No need to take,
When the willing will give.
I did not teach you to steal,
I gave you the will to live.

Rodney D. Harakal 8/26/2013

All I Could Do Was Pray

All I Could Do Was Pray

I was on the other side of the world,
When she was six months old.
All I could do was pray.
How could I be a Daddy,
When I was so far away?
I lived each day and cried at night.
I was a soldier who was ready to fight.
All I could do was pray.

She stole my heart at birth.
 I loved her for every second it was worth.
Thousands of miles away,
All I could do was pray.

After a year, 12 months of a hardship tour.
We met again and started over.
It was a new beginning.
She didn't even know me,
I was not winning.
All I could do was pray.

It didn't take long; she knew I was Dad.
I was the man who she didn't have.
Once together, we did not forget,
My baby girl, with little barrettes.
I did her hair, and we flew kites,
Went outside and rode her bike.

Cheerleader, she was,
On those cold football nights.
All I could do was pray.

Her smile is forever,
Her kindness is close to my heart.
She is a beautiful young lady.
I knew it from the start.
Her eyes were so glaring blue, hair was golden,
Voice of an Angel, her hand I was holding.
All I could do was pray...

All grown up with three beautiful girls of her own.
Wherever they sleep is where they call home.
Not rich, nor full of money, but tastefully proud.
Her pride stood tall, and her smile was so wide.
She would play in the sand, come high or low tide.

All I could do was pray.
Ailing was she, beneath the eyes to see.
To walk in her shoes,
It was not for you or me.

Her time has come.
A calling from Above.
Rainbows, Pearly Gates, and Angels,
The sky, filled with little white doves.

God came for my Angel,
And it was her time to go.
Lots of tears were shed,
There are very many more that I know.

I lost my baby girl,
Only memories that I have left.
When I gave her my last kiss,
Only God knows what was next.

She is in Heaven now,
And there she shall rest.
All I can do is Pray!

Dedicated to my daughter, I Love You, Baby Girl

Rodney D. Harakal 4/27/15

Angel

In times of trouble and times of pain,
I close my eyes and remember His name.
I look to the sky, beyond my means.
Lift my hands and I begin to scream.
My mouth opens, no words or sound.
I drop to my knees, my hands, they pound.
Nothing I do can bring her back.
All my happy thoughts I do not lack.
She is forever my angel from birth.
Every moment I cherished and retained its worth.

It's hard to fathom what the next days will bring.
With her in my heart, the glory must be.
I don't know if my reactions will justify me.
I just pray that my angel will always be with me.
As I close my eyes tonight and try to sleep,
A tear will fall as I will weep.
Goodnight, my angel, my baby girl.
I will never forget that you are my world!

I LOVE YOU, BABY GIRL

Rodney D. Harakal 12/19/2018

Angel

Arms Open Wide

Arms open wide, nobody to hold.

Hugs and kisses no more, I've been told.

Our hearts have been torn, no mending inside.

My arms are open, arms open wide.

I hold them open, hoping to hold you again.

What once was there no longer remains.

I close my eyes and only see you.

Within my arms, is it so true?

I feel your touch so close to me.

My heart pounds, no soul to see.

I folded my arms, no one to touch.

Tears in my eyes, my love for you is so much.

I can't wipe them away; each tear has a meaning.

I cry and cry, my tears, they are streaming.

I cannot stop until each memory is gone.

Every dream I have, every memory is a new one.

My heart is with you until the day I die.

Every day, even if I cry and cry.

So here I am with nothing to hide.

Here I stand, with my arms open wide.

Rodney D. Harakal 12/26/2013

From Above

It's been a long time with a smile on my face,
I'm sad, I'm Happy, what am I doing in this place?
It's not here, the physical, the home, or the nature we are in.
My mood, the state of which my mind is wondering?

Things of the past that cannot be changed
It's not the third day that He can Rise again.
Emotions run deep, thoughts on your mind.
What had been done, not much was kind.

Prayers are asked for forgiveness each night.
No answers to see, each day to foresight.
The light of day, no sun in the sky,
Darkest of clouds, makes wonders why.

Dusk till dawn, the darkness sets.
The moon will shine on the clouds as they rest.
Stars above a galaxy away,
Seeing the Heavens is where you stay.

That is where the light shall shine.
I look above the stars and the moon.
There I find that smile of mine.
Now I know what I am doing in this place.
It was you who put this smile on my face.

I know that you will not Rise again.
When you were on Earth, you were Heaven-sent.
Emotions run deep; you are always on my mind.
It was you who gave me Life to Find.

I think of you every day.
There are no clouds, just sun and rays.
From Above, I know it's you,
Looking down on me today.

Rodney D Harakal 9/17/2015

From Above

Happy Birthday

It was on this day that I first heard you cry,
This day of birth in my Angel's eyes.
Blue sky above, white clouds, white doves.
My beautiful baby from the great Lord above.

In my arms, I cuddled, I'm Dad from the start.
You, my angel, always in my heart.
Cake, ice cream, and candles are so bright,
I will burn for you each birthday night.

My daughter, Happy Birthday to You,
On June 10th, a celebration we will do.
You are in our hearts and minds.
This day, each year, will always be a special time.

Celebration!
Happy Birthday, My Angel.
We Love and Miss You so much

Rodney D Harakal 6/10/2015

Happy Birthday

My Child Grand

This Life I have is my Heaven while I am alive.
Three children of my child and Grand of mine.
Hearts of gold and Angels within,
They give me life and make it worth to live.

Sunshine of the day and stars at night,
Bring dreams to me with a shed of light.
Splendid happiness with nothing to need.
'Tis my heartbeat and planted seeds.

Fresh air is brought with every breath I take,
Longer-lasting life, for which they make.
Three little lives her seeds did expand,
This experience makes "My Child Grand."

Rodney D Harakal 8/27/2015

My Child Grand

I Am DAD

We don't carry them for nine months in a womb.
We can't feel your pain or what's inside of you.
We grow together as one.
Father and daughter or Mother and son.

As all is well in Life and Wealth.
A baby to be born in perfect Health.
We share a Love and a bond when this child arrives.
This baby helps us lead beautiful lives.
We all know that we count fingers and toes,
This baby's birth makes our eyes all aglow.

A wonderful life we want for this child.
We treat it with care and Love all the while.
The baby changes our life for all the good.
Sure, it's time for fatherhood.
We should change diapers and feed at night.
Wake up in the morning to a sunny delight.

They grow each day with a roll or crawl.
Hold their bottle, have a burp and some drool.
We Love each moment, everything they do.
Spit-up on the suit jacket, pee all over you.

Can't wait to get home from work, just so I can see,
That beautiful baby, smiling when holding onto me.
This baby is so amazing; she is all that I think about.
First thing in the morning, day in and day out.

They get older in life, and they walk and talk,
The things that come out must have been learned from us all.
We try to teach them right from wrong,
We want them to sing, glorious in song.

Not everything taught is your way or mine,
But morals and mores, they turn out just fine.
They go to school and college too.
Learn about life and be on their way soon.

They have ups and downs and turn for advice.
Hope they come to you and don't think twice.
They meet the partner of their dreams,
You have to hold back, take a breath, and make sure you don't
scream.

But they make it work, and they do okay,
Stand by their side; they will make it another day.

You are their parent, and they will always be your baby,
It is not the time; there is no maybe.
This child is yours forever and a day.
They should outlast your life; you wouldn't think without delay.

So, life goes on, Grandparent, you are.
Life is fantastic; I love it so far.
You Love your child and grandchildren as such,
Very deep in your heart, with Love is so much.

Until one day her heart is no more.
It can't take the blood that she has stored.
Her blood is thicker than water we know.
But through those arteries, there's no way it could flow.

You can say it was her time. That's easy for you to say.
I never got to see her or say I Love you, to her face.
It was too late the last time that we had spoken.
I touched her body, kissed her face, and my Princess never woke.

At that time, I felt my heart grow.
It started to beat fast, then began to slow.
It emptied first, then filled with her joy, her laughter, smile and more.
This was still my daughter, for whom I will always live for.
I know that this is so very sad.
But I am forever; I am her DAD.

Rodney D. Harakal 5/24/2015

Last Kiss

My tears of today,
I'm feeling the memories of my sorrow.
My tears of today,
Feel the pain into tomorrow.
It has been many years,
Yesterday's moon has never set.
Your Spirit of Life has not left me just yet.
I can see your eyes,
A blue color of Mother Nature's sky.
Your eyes are closed,
Looking up to the Heavens.
I feel your presence very close by.
I do not remember a day,
That I do not ask why.

With an exhale of breath,
I seek the comfort of memories that were once just mine.
I touched your hand,
I touched your cheek.
I finally had a feeling,
Where my tears and knees were weak.
I signed a cross upon your head.
Kissed you goodbye,
With my last kiss on your forehead.

Rodney D. Harakal 3/26/2020

My Link

I pray to Him,
I asked in His name,
"Oh Lord, please let her know,
I miss her today.
I think of her all the time.
My mind goes crazy,
When I get touched from behind.
My mind is a little hazy.
There is nobody there,
And I feel it in my heart.
That she is with me. Here.
Daylight through the dark."
I believe that is my link,
That is for me to know,
My daughter is with me,
From dark until the sun glows.
All day and night, I feel her on my shoulder.
Like, I can carry her.
Her wings put us at ease.
That feeling I get,
The nudge, touch, and even the little breeze.
I thought I saw her,
That was my link.

Rodney D. Harakal 3/12/2025

My Link

Our Lost Loved Ones

You must realize, they were in our lives forever,
That is where they were meant to be.
Suddenly, they were gone. Disappeared.
Out of nowhere, for only God to see.
Laid to rest, An Angel up high,
Each day, a tear, and we look to the sky.
We touched her hand and gave her a kiss.
I felt her soul, and she will be sadly missed.
I watched her leave; they took her away.
Her heart stood by, as I stared and gazed.
I felt her touch me, on my shoulder, so light,
She is still with me, in my heart, tonight.
We looked and looked, and they cannot be found.
Sometimes our heads are stuck to the ground.
It's birthday time we miss and we mourn,
Days before and after, we are all so very torn.
Death still beholds us, not a few days a year,
Every day, there is something that we shed a tear.
We will not get over it, a loss we should not have.
No words can be spoken; we will always be sad.
A celebration when we can, remembrance of Joy and Life,
My daughter, I Love You, Good Morning and Good Night!

Rodney D. Harakal 6/22/2018

Seeds

So many things are going through my head,
Some good, some bad, and some not to be said.
My head is in pain, and my heart does ache.
I hear those voices in which I do not partake.
Some say I'm crazy, that I already know.
If there is one thing I will never put on a show.
What you see is me, all day in and out.
I have cooled my way; there's no need to shout.
Mistakes we make, we shed some tears.
We learn our lessons throughout the years.
Hugs and kisses don't always fix the times that are rough.
You say goodnight and I Love You, sometimes just not enough.
What we do and what we say,
We sure do preach, and we sure do pray.
Life is so short, and we take it for granted.
We don't take enough time for the seeds that we planted.

P. S. Please take time for your seeds. Life is short.
Make all the bad good. Before you know it, they are all grown.
In some cases, they are gone.

Rodney D. Harakal 5/21/2015

Snowflake

I am unique,
Not one of the same.
I fall from the sky,
I'm true to my name.
I meet your eyes,
With a look of a stare.
Oh, how I melt,
From the beauty of your glare.
You melt me from the inside.
On the outside, I drip.
I turn into liquid,
With the heat from your lips.
Your hands touch me,
Shape me round.
You are always an angel,
Your wings are on the ground.
I look and I stare,
Your beauty is so white.
Falling from the sky,
So deep into the night.

Rodney D. Harakal 12/21/2013

Snowflake

Tears

It has been a very long few days,
But a very short lifetime.
So many things have happened.
So many more have been explored.
My eyes close, and you flash before me.
I open them, and you are no longer there.
I turn out the lights, and total darkness appears.
I can see no more,
There are so many tears.
It's total silence,
My heart is beating like a drum.
I can't feel my body,
I haven't moved,
I am numb.
I feel your presence with every breath that I take,
My heart is racing,
My tears are never to be fake.
I always told you the truth and never had to lie.
It is this very moment,
My tears will never run dry.

Rodney D. Harakal 4/23/15

What Was Meant

We get older and sometimes forget,
Who we were, and what was meant.
All grown up, and we worked so hard,
All for what? Just follow His words.
We might not know, but it doesn't make any sense.
We follow His words and know that's what was meant.
Do not ask why or what I should have done,
Ask forgiveness, you shall be mended, my son.
Look up to the sky, with open spread arms,
A sign of the cross, a smile of charm.
Who we were and what was meant,
Follow His Word, for All who were Heaven-sent.

Rodney D. Harakal 5/23/2014

Why o' Why

Why o' why, Lord, did you take her away?
I tried so hard to show her the way.
Where was it that I went wrong?
It doesn't seem right, so young and so strong.
But, why o' why, Lord, did my daughter have to die?
So many questions, and I shouldn't ask why.
I keep looking up to Him.
I go under and cannot swim.
On top of the water, I cannot tread.
So much pain, so many tears are shed.
Head hits the ground, right on your teeth,
Your feet are pulled out from underneath.

With every stride, you land on your knees.
Happy moments, you aim to please.
You try to please in every which way.
Your best is done each and every day.
It is filled with dreams, family, kids and stuff.
What you have in your heart is not enough.

What you have in your heart is not enough,
It is filled with dreams, family, kids and stuff.
Your best is done each day.

You try to please in every which way.
Happy moments, you aim to please.
With every stride, you land on your knees.
Your feet are pulled out from underneath,

Head hits the ground, right on your teeth.
So much pain, so many tears are shed,
On top of the water, I cannot tread.
I go under and cannot swim,
I keep looking up to Him.

So many questions, and I shouldn't ask why,
But, why o' why, Lord, did my daughter have to die?
It doesn't seem right, so young and so strong.
Where was it that I went wrong?
I tried so hard to show her the way.
Why o' why, Lord did you take her away?

Rodney D. Harakal 6/6/2015

Why o' Why

The Words of a Tear

When a teardrop falls, it has meaning to someone, if not all.
All those who know that tear. Is it sad or is it fear?
Wipe it away. A sleeve, a wrist, a tissue, if may.
Or does it slide down your cheek to the ground?
Your heart is fast beating, as you stand all alone.
Staring at the Earth, silence is bleeding.

The first tear is gone, and there are more to come. All alone in which silence is some.
No injury, accident or fight has occurred; it is this silence that you are getting ready to endure.
All the silence is getting so loud. Not a single soul can hear this enormous crowd.
I use my sleeve, my wrist and some tissues too. For this, silence will also happen to you.

I can hear the excitement, the roars and the screams, the hugs and the music, the kisses and the singing.
Most of all, every night and day, my silence is filled with dreams of yesterday.

And now my tears I don't wipe clean. They are filled with happiness and smiles, you see.

There is no more silence, but parties and dreams.

I talk to you every day, and though it still seems,

That our yesterdays, todays and tomorrows, our memories we have through the years.

They made for an awesome journey, through "The Words of a Tear".

Rodney D. Harakal 3/1/2016

Acknowledgment

How can I say thank you enough to all of the inspiring people and places and magical thoughts that may have had a part in helping me contribute to writing these awesome poems. My daughter Trista is the number one instrumentalist involved in this historic creative writing gesture that we have created here. My wife, Cindy Harakal, the most amazing person in the world. She contributes life to things of less fortunate abilities. Like me! My Son Jarod is so inspirational to me. He inspires me so much. He goes after what he wants to in life, and generally, he gets it. When he was in the womb, he saved my life. To find out how, I guess I will have to write another poetry book for the answer. My brother, Jerry Harakal. Another inspiration for life. His accomplishments are something that I never could have achieved. I look up to him with no blind eyes. I just may have to write a few more poetry books to let you figure out What's Happening!

I would like to thank all of my Family and friends, if there are any who inspired me to write. I have a long way to go, and if this works, there are a few more books to be written.

Thank you,

Rodney D. Harakal

To be continued...

www.ingramcontent.com/pod-product-compliance
Lightning Source LLC
Chambersburg PA
CBHW061721120626
46550CB00003B/1318